SIR LAURENCE OLIVIER IN SPAIN

The shooting of *Richard III* and other visits

MARGARIDA ARAYA

Copyright © 2016 Margarida Araya

slofanpage@gmail.com

All rights reserved. No part of this book may be reproduced or utilised in any form or by any means, electronic or mechanical, including photocopying, recording or by any information storage and retrieval system, without permission in writing from the author.

Every effort has been made to trace the copyright holders of material quoted in this book. If application is made in writing to the author, any omissions will be included in future editions.

ISBN-10: 1540786234

ISBN-13: 978-1540786234

"Of all the things I've done in life, directing a motion picture is the most beautiful. It's the most exciting and the nearest than an interpretive craftsman, such as an actor can possibly get to being a creator".

Laurence Olivier

To all who have believed in this project from the beginning and especially to Lucía, Bob, Esperanza, and the Torrelodones City Council. Special thanks also to Marilyn for her help.

Talent and magic penetrated the walls to seize Lola. And as magic can be quite mischievous, it also seized an English woman, Vivien Leigh, who danced flamenco with admirable grace and ease. Sir Lawrence [sic] didn't see this marvellous performance by his distinguished wife because he had left a little earlier. He was tired; he also had been wounded by an arrow to the leg during the battle scene he was shooting near Madrid with five hundred horses. But he was so courteous that, seeing Vivien so enthusiastic about Lola and her company, he told her to stay (Morales, 1954).

Sofía Morales –through Primer Plano film magazine– thus described a flamenco party at Florián Rey's[1] house in Madrid at the end of September 1954. Lola was the incomparable flamenco dancer Lola Flores; Vivien was the famous star of *Gone with the Wind*, and Sir Lawrence (with the common orthographic error[2]) was the distinguished British actor, director and producer Laurence Olivier.

What were Laurence Olivier and Vivien Leigh doing at a flamenco party? Had someone really shot an arrow at the famous actor in the middle of the 20th century?

One of the first foreign film shootings on Spanish soil (previous to the Samuel Bronston super productions) was the final scenes of *Richard III* that recreated the Bosworth battle. Laurence Olivier directed and starred this film.

This book will explore why Olivier chose –in his words– "those stunted Spanish trees and the silver grass" to represent an English battlefield, and how the Spanish journalists reacted to the first 'official' visit of the Olivier-Leigh couple. And despite attempts at secrecy, we will see some of the few extant images of the shooting. We will also discover some previously unknown details, for example, what 'distinguished' person lent a horse to Olivier and how

---

[1] A Spanish movie director, actor and screenwriter; very popular during the 1920s and the 1930s.
[2] The rest of "Lawrence" or "Vivian" misspellings in the quotes have been corrected to not abuse of the term 'sic'.

the newly completed Cross of the Valley of the Fallen[3] served as background for King Richard during the battle.

All the texts from the Spanish magazines and newspapers have been translated the way they were written, in an attempt to maintain the old Spanish ornate (and naive) style from the 50s.

---

[3] Funerary monument, symbol of the Franco regime.

CONTENT

1. OLIVIER AND RICHARD III 12
2. A BRIEF INITIAL CONTACT 17
3. FILM LOCATIONS FOR *RICHARD III* 22
4. THE SHOOTING OF *RICHARD III* 36
5. DALÍ'S PORTRAIT 63
6. CHRISTMAS IN ANDALUSIA 67
7. OTHERS VISITS TO SPAIN 80
8. ILLUSTRATIONS 86
9. BIBLIOGRAPHY 87
10. ABOUT THE AUTHOR 91

1. OLIVIER AND RICHARD III

William Shakespeare's *Richard III* was a key play and character in Laurence Olivier's repertoire. In September 1944, after his debut as a cinematographic director in *Henry V*, Olivier's Richard was a triumph at the New Theatre[4] in London. It was his definitive recognition as a 'great' actor.

Olivier as Richard III in 1944

---

[4] Currently, the Noel Coward Theatre.

His success was so remarkable that actor John Gielgud gifted him with a sword that had been used by Edmund Kean –another great Shakespearean actor– while playing Richard in 1813. The sword passed from hand to hand until reaching another legendary actor, Henry Irving, in 1877. Irving's lead actress and Gielgud's great aunt, Ellen Terry, passed it to Gielgud's mother, Kate Terry, who recommended him to hand it to another "youngster with promise". So Gielgud did it, solemnly, in a parade from Haymarket to the New Theatre. A couple of months later, *Henry V* was released to cinema, and Olivier's reputation was fixed in the firmament of the big stars.

But *Richard III* didn't disappear after that season. The play became part of the European Tour repertory of the Old Vic at the end of the war in 1945. Some years later, in 1948, after shooting his award-winning *Hamlet*, Olivier took the character on an Old Vic tour of several months' duration around Australia and New Zealand. His wife Vivien Leigh, after recovering from tuberculosis, played Lady Anne.

In 1949, Richard was resurrected during a brief and final revival of the play at the New Theatre. It was Olivier's final season at the Old Vic.

In 1953, the Oliviers had a great theatrical success with *The Sleeping Prince*, which some years later would become the film *The Prince and the Showgirl*. But Olivier didn't want to give up his Shakespearian filmmaking, and he decided to turn to his most memorable theatrical character. He wrote to his son Tarquin (from his first marriage to Jill Esmond): "*Richard III* is ON. So you can imagine there is no spare moment for me now. It's OK. I intend enjoying it. I am sick of suffering under things and letting them make me unhappy." (Coleman, 2005).

Unable to secure funding from Filippo Del Giudice –who had produced his previous Shakespearean films– Olivier financed the movie through his own company, Laurence Olivier Productions (LOP) with further assistance from Alexander Korda, the Hungarian producer and director; a big shot in the British cinematographic industry. *Richard III* was Korda's last production.

For the screen version, Olivier used his theatre script, in which he had cut and reorganized the original text, adding fragments of *Henry VI Part III* to the *Richard III* version adapted by Colley Cibber in 1700. As he had done previously, he based his performance on two men: Vocally, he was inspired by recollections of veteran actors on how Irving sounded on the stage, and physically, he copied the look of the American theatrical producer Jed Harris.

Olivier as Richard III in 1955

After courting some great names –and friends– like Richard Burton, Robert Donat, Michael Redgrave, and John Mills, Olivier finally settled on Cedric Hardwicke, John Gielgud and Ralph Richardson for the main roles. The three actors, together with Olivier, formed a respectable quartet of British knights. Richardson had played Richmond in Olivier's stage version, but now he would play Buckingham. The Lady Anne role went to Claire Bloom, and Esmond Knight, portraying Ratcliff, was the main character in one of the scenes during the Spanish filming. Knight has the honour of being the only actor appearing in all films directed by Olivier.

William Walton composed the soundtrack, and other regular members of Olivier's crew, such as Roger Furse (Production Design) and Carmen Dillon (Art Direction), reprised their roles. Norman Hargood should also be mentioned here because he was the photographer who took the only existing stills of the *Richard III* shoot in Spain. Unlike other foreign productions in those days – Orson Welles' *Mr. Arkadin* (1955) and Stanley Kramer's *The Pride and the Passion* (1957)— access was forbidden to all Spanish journalists and photographers, so everything was done in great secrecy.

The first part of this book –based on information from Spanish newspaper libraries and Olivier biographies and essays– compiles existing information on the *Richard III* shooting in the Madrid environs. Miraculously, this geographic region has barely changed in sixty years, but until now it hasn't shared its secrets about this shoot.

2. A BRIEF INITIAL CONTACT

The shooting of the film *Richard III* began in Spain on 12th September 1954 with the end, the Bosworth battle, and it continued for three more months at the Shepperton Studios in England.

In 1944, due to the war, Olivier travelled to Ireland to film the Battle of Agincourt from *Henry V* to have sufficient men and horses at his disposal. This time, Tony Bushell –Olivier's usual Associate Producer– told him about a perfect spot in Spain, a sunny place where they wouldn't suffer delays due to the Irish rain and where they would be "*far from the pylons and vapour trails of England.*" (Olivier, 1992)

Two valuable documents indicate that Olivier had a brief initial contact with the zone destined to become the locale of the shooting in June 1954. The first-hand confirmation comes from the Olivier diaries –housed at the British Library in London– where we find the first mention of Spain on 20th June 1954: On that morning Olivier flew to Madrid and visited the Manzanares, El Escorial and Pardo areas with the Spanish producer Luis Roberts. Roberts was in charge of cinematographic business in Madrid –especially the Arthur Rank films– and he was the Location Associate Producer in *Richard III*. Olivier went back to London on the morning of 21st June.

On two later occasions, Olivier declared to the press that he had been in Spain earlier incognito. A trail of a photograph that appeared in a book about Marilyn Monroe led us to the discovery of a Spanish magazine that had done an exhaustive coverage of that unknown first visit.

It was the journalist Alfredo Tocildo (from Triunfo magazine) and his inseparable photographer Miguel Ángel Basabe who got –after a tenacious wait– exclusive access. They were the only journalists who documented Laurence Olivier's first official visit to Spain.

The fully detailed account of Olivier's brief visit appears in the article entitled "*Good morning Sir! - Laurence Olivier spends 19 hours in Madrid, from plane to plane*" published on 23rd June 1954.

In the piece, Tocildo relates that on 12th June he received a tip about Olivier's immediate arrival in Madrid. He knew that Olivier was playing *The Sleeping Prince* on stage, so he calculated that Olivier could only travel on Sundays (the "dark" day in English theatres). On 13th June, Sunday, the B.E.A. (British European Airways) plane form London landed in Madrid but Olivier was not inside.

On the following Sunday, 20th June, Tocildo went back to Barajas Airport, but the B.E.A plane had arrived early, at 14:30. And although Olivier wasn't on the passenger list, he was indeed on the plane. At customs, the journalist was able to see Olivier's passport since, according to regulations in those days, passports were left there in custody. Tocildo discovered that Olivier's baggage consisted of a very small suitcase and a toiletries bag. The tip had also indicated him that the actor would stay at the Wellington Hotel. The hotel confirmed the reservation and revealed that someone had sent Olivier a large arrangement of flowers, but Olivier never appeared at that hotel. Tocildo didn't give up as he knew he had one last hope: to 'catch' him at Barajas Airport, on his return to England. He checked the list of flights and noticed that the first flight to London, a Spanish Iberia flight, would depart the following day at 9:30. He arrived at the airport without much hope, but his tenacity was rewarded: At 8:35 Laurence Olivier appeared at Barajas Airport. Tocildo's first impression of Olivier was that he was shorter, blonder, nicer, and politer than he expected --but that he didn't like journalists at all.

> I've come to Madrid –my first time here– to briefly look for some location shots for my next film, *Richard III*. I'm going to direct and star in the film at the beginning of September. It will be in Technicolor, and with the new Cinemascope process, Paramount's exclusive. I've just seen some admirable tests of it in London. (Tocildo, 1954)

Olivier told the journalist about all his activities the day before. After arriving at the airport, Olivier got into a 1947 Ford and went directly to the historic castle in the Manzanares region. He explained to Tocildo that some battle scenes would take place in front of the castle (although the castle never appeared in the movie). From there he went to El Campillo –a state near El Escorial– where he took notes and photographs and made sketches. He came back to the hotel –the Palace– at 21:30, where he secluded himself in his room and continued working. He chose Villa Rosa –a popular flamenco venue in Spain– to have dinner because he wanted to see, amongst other things, the dancer Faíco. It seems that Olivier and his wife were a flamenco dance enthusiasts; they never missed Antonio shows in London. He left the restaurant at two o'clock in the morning and had gotten up at 7 a.m. that morning.

After other questions about theatre and cinema, Tocildo asked him if any Spaniard would participate in the movie; Olivier answered that it wasn't a certain thing yet. As it turned out, only members of the Spanish army participated as extras in the battle. About the length of the shooting, Olivier declared it would take "as long as it takes". He didn't want to specify if it would take four, five or six months, and he added that, in the middle of July, he would come back with his wife to work directly on the site, but that he would shoot the interior scenes in London.

Luis Roberts, the Spanish producer and collaborator in this film who was with Olivier, ended the interview, telling the journalist that the actor was tired. (Roberts, together with his brother and Anthony Bushell, were the ones who had had dinner with Olivier the previous day). Finally, after the classic question about what had impressed him the most about Spain, Olivier answered:

> The sun, the sun... and that Castile[5] dust. Look at me; look at my poor eyes... (Tocildo, 1954).

---

[5] Spanish historical region next to Madrid. All the film shooting areas are now part of the Community of Madrid.

Olivier waits at Barajas Airport

3. FILM LOCATIONS FOR *RICHARD III*

The first mention of the shooting in the Spanish press appeared in ABC newspaper on 5th August: "(London Films) will film in Spain a terrific horse fight: the battle from the film *Richard III*, which Sir Laurence Olivier is going to direct as well as star in. 'In Spain, we have found –they have told us– the horses we need, the riders we require and the light.'"

It is clear, then, that weather and horses were the reasons for choosing Spain.

In August 1954, the Oliviers spent some holiday weeks in Portofino (Italy), at Rex Harrison and Lily Palmer's home and the Italian paparazzi promptly reported it. On 12th August, after a brief return to London, they landed at Barajas Airport in a B.E.A. flight.

On 13th August news of their arrival appeared in briefs from different Spanish newspapers:

> London 12 - Sir Laurence Olivier and his wife, the actress Vivien Leigh, have flown to Madrid to prepare the shooting of some scenes for the *Richard III* film. (EFE, 1954)

> This afternoon the British cinema actor Sir Laurence Olivier has arrived from London, with his wife, the unforgettable star of *Gone with the Wind*, Vivien Leigh. Sir Laurence Olivier will direct –he is also the star and the producer– some scenes of the film *Richard III* in El Escorial. (La Vanguardia, 1954)

Typical photographs of them next to the plane accompanied these notices, so it is clear that this time the Spanish press was indeed alerted to their arrival. There is also, from ABC newspaper, an image of the couple in an indeterminate place next to some flamenco postcards, probably a newsstand from the airport.

Sir Laurence Olivier in Spain

The producer Luis Roberts —as in the June visit— welcomed them. After dealing with the press, they went to their hotel. Journalist Vic Rueda, in his article for Primer Plano magazine, disclosed that, at the airport, the journalists were given the name of a different hotel (just to give them the slip). But it was useless; some hours later everybody knew where they were staying.

It is likely that the Oliviers stayed at the luxurious Ritz Hotel. Two hints point to that conclusion: first, some images of the couple — taken by La Actualidad Española magazine— walking around the Prado Museum gardens (which are next to the hotel) and their choice, in 1957, of the Ritz Hotel for a short stay in Madrid[6]. Unfortunately, because the Ritz does not have records from that time, we cannot be certain. George Marquet, the owner of the Ritz and Palace Hotels, didn't want to accommodate 'artists' in his hotels, but *De Madrid al cine* (a book about Madrid film locations, which doesn't mention the shooting of *Richard III*) notes some exceptions made to Marquet's rule: "Sir Laurence Olivier made use of his status as Knight of the Queen of England to get a room" (De Madrid al cine, 2003).

On 13th August, before visiting the filming zone, the couple had a brief encounter with La Actualidad Española magazine, mentioned above. But it wasn't an interview, just a graphic meeting; the only 'new' information found in the article is that Vivien Leigh liked to keep her sunglasses on until late afternoon and that Laurence Olivier didn't like to be photographed without his jacket.

> The "secrecy" of their trip, at least during the first days of their stay in Spain, doesn't help us to find out the reason they are here. Sir Laurence's intention was to visit El Escorial, where he will choose some location shots for his next film, *Richard III*, which will have them in the leading roles. On the other hand, Mrs. Olivier seems quite recovered from her illness; that disease called by a certain newspaper "the illness of the century": the nervous breakdown. (Lozano, 1954)

---

[6] See chapter 6. Christmas in Andalusia.

Cover of La Actualidad Española

That evening —their last night in Madrid— the Oliviers were seen by different journalists having dinner with Roberts at the popular restaurant Riscal, which attracted international stars with its *paellas*.

Vic Rueda described, in Primer Plano, the meeting:

> I tried to communicate with them at the hotel, but it was impossible. I didn't worry much and one night I was at the Riscal's terrace, with my friend and colleague Miguel Pérez Ferrero, when the couple arrived to have the classic paella.

They were so near that I didn't want to miss the opportunity. My friend Pérez Ferrero and I went to their table to greet them, and I got what I wanted: to chat a little bit with them.

They come from Italy, where they have spent some days in the Italian Riviera with another couple of British actors who summer there, [Rex] Harrison and Lily Palmer. They have had a great time there, and now they have come to Spain —he had already visited Spain not so long ago— because he wanted his wife to know this wonderful place. I told them I had searched for them in vain. They mentioned the reasons why they don't give interviews. What a pity! I think actors have a duty with their popularity. But the important thing is that despite their refusal, we could see them. (....) I was very happy to hear that Vivien is getting well. I remembered that the last time she went to Hollywood she suffered such a breakdown that she couldn't finish her movie. Later, in London, she also had to leave the stage to rest. Now, probably, with the Italian and Spanish fresh air she will be fully recovered very soon. Due to their behaviour, they reminded me of another English couple: James Mason and Pamela [Kellino]; he is a good actor but not as excellent as Laurence Olivier.

When we left the table, and we wished them good night, I asked them to take a photo. They gently accepted, but they preferred to have the photographs taken at the exit. We did it this way.

Then, we came back to our table, and they left the restaurant very soon. Someone said: "It's Vivien Leigh! She's very small!" And the only answer I can give is: "Yes, but she did *Gone with the Wind*". What a wonderful couple of actors!

The Oliviers sign autographs before leaving the Riscal restaurant

The ABC journalist and critic Donald (pseudonym of Miguel Pérez Ferrero, mentioned by Vic Rueda) also spoke to them at the Riscal. Through his brief interview, he learned –for the first time– the exact place of the future shooting, El Campillo. Thus, they were not going to shoot at the monastery of El Escorial —as the media would continue to report during the following days— but on a land near the town of El Escorial. Vivien Leigh showed her wide cultural knowledge:

> Vivien Leigh is talkative. She quickly asked me if we read a lot of Shakespeare in Spain, and I said yes, although a little more of Cervantes. She told me that Thurston Wilder was carefully studying Lope de Vega in order to publish a work about him. Then she asked me about a Spanish writer: "Azorín".
>
> - I would like to meet him.

I promised to introduce him to her on the 28th when the couple returns to start filming the location shots of *Richard III*. They won't film at the monastery of El Escorial —because it would be illogical— but at El Campillo.

- Why are these exterior scenes going to be shot in Spain?

- Very easy, because we gain time. In England, it would take months and months of shooting. We want the sun. The landscape is wonderful. The weather. Do you get it?

Laurence Olivier remains silent while his wife keeps talking. She knows about Lope and García Lorca's theatre. She suddenly says.

- You have a great theatrical tradition!

It is pleasant to respond:

- Yes, we undoubtedly have a very important drama tradition.

Laurence Olivier and Vivien Leigh are leaving today, but they will come back soon. At the end of the month, they will be here again. They have come to Spain somewhat incognito, like Royals on their way; in fact, they are royals in the universal art of acting. And they want to tell us "see you soon" in silence, but kindly. In a corner of the crowded terrace, they tried to go unnoticed, and they nearly achieved it. Only the wonderful and penetrating green eyes of the great actress betrayed them. When people started to notice them, they said "goodbye", and they left (Donald, 1954).

In 1966, Donald met Olivier again after the *Othello* film premiere in London, and he reminded him about that brief interview in Madrid:

> D – Some years ago, Laurence Olivier, we invaded you in a Madrilenian terrace (...). Now we try to invade you again, on this day that is also quite memorable.

> LO – I remember now that invasion. The Madrilenian summer was ending. From that terrace, you could see the happy winks of the multicolour city lights. We liked to think that those winks were special greetings to us (Donald, 1966).

There is also an image of the Oliviers at the famous cocktail bar Museo Chicote, an almost compulsory visit for all the stars who travelled to Madrid in those days. The date of the photograph is unknown, but it was probably taken during this brief stay.

The Oliviers with Pedro Chicote

On 14th August, the same day that the Oliviers left Spain, some newspaper briefs already mentioned San Lorenzo del Escorial as the shooting location. In addition, the Sevillian edition of ABC provided an anecdote that didn't appear in any other medium:

> Madrid 13. The cinema stars Sir Laurence Olivier and his wife, Vivien Leigh, went shopping in Madrid. Sir Laurence bought a pair of wellingtons and a pair of trousers. After putting on both garments he went out into the street. The Oliviers are very

happy visiting in Madrid, and they praise its beauty. (CIFRA, 1954)

On 15th August, La Vanguardia reported the couple's return to London. Before they caught the plane, they gave one last interview —at the restaurant in Barajas Airport— to Fotogramas cinema magazine, which would appear some days later:

> They departed for London, but they will come back to Madrid very soon. The location shots of *Richard III*, with a script by Laurence Olivier, will be filmed at the Campillo state, near El Escorial. Laurence Olivier will direct and star.
> Not so long ago Sir Laurence Olivier was in Madrid incognito. Now, with his wife, the world-famous Vivien Leigh, he has done something similar. They registered at the hotel under a pseudonym, and it was really difficult to find them. On Saturday, when the famous couple was departing for London, we had the chance to speak with them quietly.
> Vivien Leigh —whose beauty and sweetness are beyond any adjective— as well as her husband Sir Laurence Olivier, answered all our questions. Sometimes the actor answered with a gesture or just by saying "There's no answer." We concluded that Sir Laurence Olivier is as secretive as they say...
> The wonderful Vivien Leigh and her husband are sitting at the airport bar, where they have had lunch. Mr. Roberts —a Spanish collaborator in the film— accompanies them, along with an English man unknown to us. We have the impression that nobody has noticed them. When Francisco Salgado takes the first shots, the "autograph hunters" start to get closer, and they even ask us for our fountain pen... It's half past two in the afternoon when we introduce ourselves. A smile from Vivien Leigh rewards us for the three days of research, nerves and phone calls.
> - Mrs. Leigh, we have been told that you have been all these days in El Escorial.

- No, —she sweetly answers— we haven't been at El Escorial. We didn't have to time to see the Monastery... Imagine that!
- We went mad looking for you everywhere...
- We have been in a state called Campillo, near El Escorial. It is the place where the *Richard III* exteriors will be shot. You know that all the exterior scenes will be shot in Spain.
- Why are you going to shoot the *Richard III* exteriors in Spain, Mrs. Leigh?
- Because of the weather. There is a wonderful sun here which is unknown in England.

We wouldn't exaggerate at all if we said that Vivien Leigh breathes stylishly. She wears a grey dress, with a brooch, a pearl wrap bracelet, and rings on both hands. Her husband only wears a big seal ring on his left little finger. Grey suit, black hat, gentleman look, but a sleepy gentleman...

Vivien Leigh –with beautiful and shining eyes-- has moved the fruit plate aside, she grabs the paper and she signs an autograph for Fotogramas. She gives us back the fountain pen and the paper; she smiles.
- With my best wishes to the Spanish people— she says.
- Would you tell us, Mrs Leigh, who is the world's best movie director?
- The world's best director is my husband.
- Do you have children?
- I have a girl and the gentleman –she points Sir Laurence– another one[7] [sic].
- When did you leave Hollywood?
- I left Hollywood in 1951.
- What is your last film?
- *A Streetcar Named Desire*.

The onlookers and the "autograph hunters" nearly push us out of the way. We approach Sir Laurence Olivier, who is sitting in front of us.

He answers our questions, and he listen to us, but with a withdrawn air, as if he were thinking about something else.

---

[7] At that time, Laurence Olivier had a boy, Tarquin, from his first marriage.

- Sir, *Richard III* is a British film or a joint production with Spain?
- It's a British film.
- Will there be Spanish actors in the film?
- Yes, but I can't give you names; also, they won't be stars.
- Who has written the script?
- The script is mine, based on the Shakespeare play.
- Could you tell us which actor has assimilated better your direction?
- There's no answer.
- Thank you, sir. We know that some international actors will be in the film, and we'd like to know who they are.
- I can't tell you that, it hasn't been decided yet.
- Personally, which do you prefer, cinema or theatre?
- I like to direct films and perform in theatre. You must bear in mind that cinema is where the director can develop himself whereas, in theatre, it's the actor who does it.

Sir Laurence Olivier starts blinking a lot. We believe he hasn't slept much. He almost involuntary closes his eyes and he listens and answers as if he were far away.

- What is your most gratifying film?
- *Henry V*, but my best work is *Hamlet*.
- When are you coming back to Spain?
- Probably on 1st September. My wife will come on the 10th or 15th.
- Will Vivien Leigh have a role in this film?
- Probably, but it's not certain.
- What are the necessary qualities to be a good film director?
- There is no answer.
- Can you tell us about the third dimension, Sir Laurence?

He looks at us, he makes a strange gesture, and then, he says unwillingly:

- That's on formation period.
- Will it have a future?

He shrugs his shoulders, and he does another of those strange gestures.

- Tell us, Sir, is it cheaper to shoot in Spain than in England?

He shrugs his shoulders again and makes a signal to the waiter but, in fact, it is as if he were telling us that he's too sleepy –that the interview is over.

Then, we talk again to Vivien Leigh.

- One last question, Mrs. Leigh. What has impressed you most on this trip?

- We didn't have much time to see things; I liked everything a lot and for this reason I hope and I want to come back... My best memory is our visit to the Prado Museum. It was unforgettable. I like Spain very much; I know the country through books and theatre.

The waiter arrives with the bill; Vivien Leigh lights a cigarette. She is the first one to stand up; then the English man and then Mr Roberts. Sir Laurence Olivier is the last one to rise, after pulling down his hat. But as soon as he stands up, he takes it off again.

Marisa Prados and Alberto Ruschel, the Brazilian film couple, approach them, and they talk for a while. They bid farewell. Close to the plane steps, Sir Laurence Olivier forces a smile and they both wave their hand to say goodbye.

At the airport, Sir Laurence Olivier broke his silence to talk to Fotogramas readers. We're waiting to face *Richard III* soon so the interview will be more... bearable. Vivien Leigh combines an exquisite beauty and elegance with an unusual charm.

Barajas Transoceanic Airport, 14th August 15:30 (Andresco, 1954)

The Oliviers chat with the Fotogramas journalist

Finally, on 25th August, El Mundo Deportivo newspaper reported the upcoming shooting in San Lorenzo del Escorial, and announced that the Oliviers would come back in September.

4. THE SHOOTING OF *RICHARD III*

We shot the battle scene in Spain, and those stunted Spanish trees and the silver grass were not Bosworth. When Richard [III] insisted on a view of his battlefield, I was forced to use a painted picture of Leicestershire with the trees a little less stunted. Who has the faintest idea what Bosworth Field looks like except people who live near Bosworth, and they're not mediaeval? (Olivier L., 1986).

Map of the zone with the towns to be mentioned encircled in red

Not a single newspaper or magazine reported on Olivier's return – together with the entire film crew— but it was, indeed, recorded in his personal diary. He arrived on 1st September in Madrid from Heathrow, on B.E.A. flight 118. Vivien Leigh, who was spending some time in Paris and Italy with friends, would not arrive until two weeks later. That day he had lunch with Tony Bushell and stayed at the La Berzosa Hotel, which was close to Torrelodones. Today, the building is part of Nebrija University.

The former La Berzosa Hotel today

DATES AND LOCATIONS

The shooting took a little over a month. In October 1954, it appeared the first mention of the Oliviers' presence in Spain. But there was a total information blackout during the shooting. A year later, in a Primer Plano article about Claire Bloom –the female star of *Richard III*-- the reason was revealed: The shoot proceeded "with locations in Spain and without giving permission to the Spanish journalists and photographers to cover the film...". (Primer Plano, 1955)

In addition, Fotogramas merely mentioned the shoot on 3rd September, when they named Claire Bloom as Olivier's co-star in the film "which will be partially filmed in Spain".

Filming permits would have been a very valuable aid in identifying the location sites but, unfortunately, no records exist. Torrelodones City Council informed us that written permits were not established until the 1970s. The present bylaws and local taxes didn't exist in the 50s. So, in those days only an oral permit was required –there wasn't any register– and the police were only to be alerted if some action in the zone were required.

The only attempt by the Spanish press to approach the filming zone was described in a 1959 article, published by ABC newspaper, about Olivier:

> At La Berzosa, two nice and intelligent journalists attempted to interview them. One of them, Sara Hostos McCormick, tried to use her status as Vivien's old schoolmate at Roehampton. However, the great actress of the big green eyes just said, shrugging her shoulders: "I don't remember." Sir Laurence remained silent, supporting his wife, and the last sentence was uttered by María Luz Nachón, playing gracefully with words: "*Sir* or not *Sir*, that is the question[8]". (ABC, 1959)

---

[8] The translation of "To be" in Spanish ("ser") has a similar sound to "Sir".

Thus, two points of the "secret" shooting are located: El Campillo (mentioned in the August interviews and in Olivier's diary, as we'll see later) and La Berzosa. And we have also a comment made by the Spanish cinema producer Teddy Villalba. In an interview, two years before his death, he explained that when the American filmmakers arrived, he "had already worked with Laurence Olivier here, at the Galapagar [Madrid] bends, on *Richard III*" (Pita, 2007).

The former Silver Screen Spain website (dedicated to registering all the foreign movies shot in Spain) provided a commentary by the late John Cabrera —from the photography department. He specified that Bosworth was, in fact, a bull field and that they had to chase the animals out on more than one occasion. Cabrera also stated that Olivier was a true gentleman.

Hence, the production moved around Torrelodones. The Spanish critic who saw the movie at the London premiere confirmed it:

> Then, we witness the Bosworth battle, filmed in Torrelodones. It is difficult to imagine those Wars of the Roses in a panorama of spaced olive trees on Castilian lands (ABC, 1955).

Tarquin Olivier received a couple of postcards in October 1954 while he was in military service. The first one was "from Bosworth Field with a Spanish stamp: Torrelodores [sic], a bull farm close to Madrid":

> This place is rich in so many beautiful ways and our location is a dream place. I wanted a tapestry-like background. I certainly got it. (Olivier T., 1992)

The second one featured Escorial's Hall of Battles, with the plumed and helmeted checkerboard of infantry and cavalry regiments:

> I have attempted to copy the picture overleaf in one or two battle shots though I don't suppose anyone will know it. The work has been really gruelling and not as unlike yours at present as you might think, but satisfactory and I am happy

with it. Baba [Vivien] has been with me almost all the time. (Olivier T., 1992)

Detail of the Higueruelas Battle from the Hall of Battles in El Escorial

The book "El Hollywood español" [The Spanish Hollywood] also mentions Galapagar and El Escorial as the locations where the battle was filmed.

In the Comparative section, there are three pairs of photographs: snapshots from the movie and photographs taken in the zone in April 2012. The first pair shows the presence of the Cross of the Valley of the Fallen, finished, precisely, in September 1954, during the shooting of *Richard III*. It is possible that the crew noticed it since a drawing of the cross appears in Olivier's diary. Given that no one has mentioned this detail before, we assume that no critic or spectator noticed the cross while viewing the film.

TECHNICAL DETAILS

Regarding the technical details of the shooting, we know from Olivier's own words that the rain had not yet arrived by September, so the grass was still "silver" due to the summer sun. This grass could not represent the green English landscape, so a green transparency —clearly seen in the movie— was added in front of the camera lens to shoot the first sequence in Spain. Olivier knew that he couldn't repeat his Agincourt battle from *Henry V*; so, he tried to get the feel of a medieval tapestry (the one he saw at El Escorial) as a visual counterpoint to Shakespeare's poetry.

The filming of the battle required eight hundred extras. Amongst them, five hundred men were recruited from the Spanish army: They were cheap and easy-to-direct extras. Although they didn't speak English, when Olivier spoke with his calm voice, the whole crew stopped to listen to him.

The only Spanish collaborator in the film, besides Teddy Villalba, was Francisco Prósper. Prósper was a Fine Arts graduate from Valencia who in the 40s started to work in the Cea Film Studios. Afterwards, he went to the Sevilla Film Studios[9] where he worked as a Set Designer. After his *Richard III* collaboration, he worked on most of the English-language productions shot in Spain (such as *Mr. Arkadin*, *Spartacus*, *Cromwell,* and *Robin and Marian*). Later on, Prósper would create his own company, working on special effects and directing some films.

---

[9] Cinema studios in Madrid, closed during the 70s.

ANECDOTES DURING THE SHOOTING

John Cottrell's biography of Olivier includes some anecdotes about the shooting, for example, the extras' organization.

Olivier wanted Bernard Hepton and John Greenwood, two young actors recruited to take charge of the swordplay, to arrange a battle scene with eight hundred extras. According to Hepton, the opposing armies were comprised mainly of Spanish extras who didn't understand English. The camera, placed on a twenty-foot tower, was positioned to point down onto the archers, panning over the foot soldiers. Then the camera had to go across to Lord Stanley's men deserting to the side of Richmond at a crucial point in the conflict. Hepton and Greenwood had organized the armies into groups of three and four soldiers, and they taught them four sword cuts and parries. They rehearsed several times while instructors called out through megaphones, "one, two, three, four". At one point, Olivier came bounding down the tower steps and slapped Hepton on the back. "That's good", he said. "Just right and now Willie Walton's got to write some music to this, so could we have them do it all again –in rhythm?". Hepton continues:

> Tony Bushell warned us at the start not to expect Sir Laurence to react to suggestions, but he explained that he was always alert to the good ideas and would absorb what you said to him even if he didn't appear to. What irritated him were people trying to press ideas upon him. Well, I have boned up on Richard III and knew that his favourite weapon was a battle axe that he used with his right arm and with all his strength. When I suggested this to him, he seemed to look right through me, paying no attention. But two days later he came back enthusiastically. "Lovely idea. Get a battle axe." So we had one made in Madrid, and when it arrived it was terrible –like a toy tomahawk. Sir Laurence was livid. The only time I saw him lose his temper (Cottrell, 1975).

Esmond Knight –who liked to refer to Richard III as "Dickie Three Eyes"– was a veteran actor and the only one who participated in all the four films directed by Olivier. He was not greatly impressed by the filming of the battle sequences.

Olivier, as Richard III, centre, directs the troops

One terrible mistake was the armour –made of rubber so that you could see it bend in close shots. All Richard's men were in dark, blackish armour, and Richmond's men were in whitish armour that made them look rather like the Tin Man in The Wizard of Oz. And then there was all that pantomime with the horses. Once Olivier was sitting on his white mare – Richard surveying the drawn-up forces of Richmond. From some trees behind him, three gauleiters ride up to the king: Catesby, Ratcliff and Lovel, you know –'The Cat, the Rat and Lovel the Dog, rule all England under the Hog'. Well, Laurence was worried because we were about to lose the light as the sun neared the mountain range. He shouted orders to us to get on with it, ride through the trees and pull up behind him. So we thundered up immediately behind him. But my horse was a stallion and being possessed of its natural instincts he promptly mounted Laurence's white mare, practically engulfing the king in the act.

"Get off, Ned, you bloody twit", he shouted.

"It's not me", I protested. "It's this randy stallion".

Then the grooms rushed in to pull the stallion off. And as I fell off backwards, somebody shouted, "Castrate that damned horse". (Cottrell, 1975)

Olivier was an accomplished horseman. There is a photograph of the actor during a break riding his beautiful mare which, according to the press note on the photo, had been lent by "Mr. Gimenex Cortés from Madrid". The Spanish Education Minister of that time – Joaquín Ruiz-Giménez Cortés– had been born in one state of La Berzosa. Thus, due to the similarity of the surnames and the vicinity it is likely that Olivier rode a horse belonging to a Minister of Franco himself.

Olivier uses a break from the shooting to ride his horse

But not all actors are good riders and to avoid losing a part, if asked, they all say they can learn to ride before the shooting starts. John Laurie –'Lovel' in the film– though married to a fine horsewoman, wasn't a rider. Dressed as his character, with a sword dangling at his side, he was instructed to take a few trial rides so that they could see how the sensitive Spanish horses reacted to a rider in a flashy medieval costume. After cantering a short distance, the actor's horse broke into a spirited gallop. Laurie's wife had advised him to saw on the horse's mouth if he had such an emergency. He did. The horse only went faster, leaping over ditches with the frail-looking fifty-seven-year-old actor hanging on for dear life. Finally, the animal stopped short at a wide ditch but Laurie didn't. He somersaulted over the horse's head and crashed into the rock-hard ground. He was carried back to the camp in a jeep, unconscious.

Afterwards, I discovered what went wrong. A Spaniard explained that their horses have very sensitive sides. The hanging sword was the cause, gently tickling the horse, and the faster it went the more strongly the irritation spurred it on. After that, we all thrust our swords through our belts, so they stayed solid. (Cottrell, 1975)

And here is the most famous anecdote about an incident that took place during the shooting, mentioned in many books:

Olivier wanted a film shot of an archer shooting Richard's horse (hence the king loses his mount and exclaims "My kingdom for a horse"). A British archer was brought especially for this job. Apparently, he was quite vain; he boasted of getting a lot of archery championships, so the crew –according to John Cabrera– started to provoke him. At the crucial moment, as the archer shot, Olivier was driving his horse up the hill, and he moved his left leg back. His armour was made of rubber –as Esmond Knight noted– and it wouldn't stop a paper dart. The arrow embedded deeply in his calf and there, in the middle of the Spanish field, the whole troop of soldiers started gradually to halt. Everybody remained silent while Olivier was still sitting in the saddle, impassive, with his leg bleeding. When Tony Bushell, the associate director, ran to him, Olivier simply asked, "*Do we have it in the can*". "*Yes*", said Bushell. Olivier, still on his horse, discussed how they could use the shot. Only after a couple of minutes talking about work he finally said: "*Now get me off the bloody horse and look for a doctor!*"

An English make-up artist and a Spanish doctor were the ones who extracted the arrow. Dr Torroba worked for the cinema studios Sevilla Films, and in 1958, attended Tyrone Power in his final moments in Madrid.

The arrow shot is perfectly visible in the film –Olivier left the scene untouched– and on the cover of this book. *Luckily* he got the wound in his left leg, Richard's lame leg. For this reason, in all the following scenes shot in London, the king's limp was real.

THE OLIVIERS IN SPAIN

The Spanish press mentioned the arrow shot briefly in one article, so it didn't go unnoticed (we will see it further on). And if the shooting was secretive, the Oliviers' presence in Spain was as well. We know they stayed at La Berzosa hotel thanks to Olivier's mention in his diary. In addition, we have evidence of two social activities the couple engaged in separately. One was the inevitable visit to the bullring, dated 9th September:

> Sir Laurence Olivier is in Spain to put the final touches on the film he's going to shoot here, *Richard III*. He is like all our visitors who quickly become fascinated with our national spectacle and come to the bullring and watch attentively. Here we see Sir Laurence carefully watching the bullfight from a barrier and happy to receive a toast from the noble figure of Antonio Bienvenida, the bullfighter. (Primer Plano, 1954)

Olivier at the bullring

The other event exemplifies the differences the couple had. While Olivier was a workaholic, Leigh was a social butterfly, always ready for the next party, no matter what time it was. The date of the article (October 3rd) indicates that the arrow incident probably happened at the end of September.

Florián Rey was sitting quietly in his garden. It was midnight. There was silence, starlight and a lot of geranium perfume. Suddenly the telephone rang in the distance, like a nickel cricket inside the house. It was Lola Flores, in a big hurry, saying: "Are you there? Good, I'm coming with my people". Her people were all her flamenco company and, amongst them, Florián Rey discovered Vivien Leigh and Laurence Olivier. In the beginning, Florián confused Vivien with Conchita Montes[10] –they bear a slight resemblance. Amongst the hodgepodge of Lola's friends –everybody in the world was there– there were also Olivier's assistant director and his wife. Edgar Neville[11] and Rafael Ortega[12] and other guests arrived later, such as Miguel Ligero[13]. First, they were all in the garden. The night was beautiful and deep, but cold for the flamencos, and the garden started to get lonely. It is known that flamenco requires walls, and it is better if the room is not very big. This way the flamenco heat cannot escape and that tight ring brings together talent and magic.

And talent and magic penetrated the walls to seize Lola. And as magic can be quite mischievous it also seized an English woman, Vivien Leigh, who danced flamenco with admirable grace and ease. Sir Laurence didn't see this marvellous performance by his distinguished wife because he had left a little earlier. He was tired; he also had been wounded by an arrow to the leg during the battle scene he was shooting near Madrid with five hundred horses. But he was so courteous that, seeing Vivien so enthusiastic about Lola and her company, he told her to stay.

Florián improvised –with his very own talent– drinks and tasty tapas and sandwiches. Vivien Leigh didn't drink Manzanilla sherry nor whisky but brandy and soda.

---

[10] Spanish actress.
[11] Spanish playwright and film director.
[12] Spanish bullfighter.
[13] Spanish actor.

Lola danced and sang until half past four, exclusively invoking all the night's magic in the honour of the famous English star (Morales, 1954).

Lola Flores and Vivien dance under the watchful eye of Edgar Neville

And here is the only article directly related to the filming –without saying anything new– which appeared in ABC newspaper on 6th October. It is also the last reference to the shooting or the Oliviers in Spain.

> "Somewhere in Spain", and in Castilian lands, the screen stars and well-known theatrical actors Vivien Leigh and Laurence Olivier have been filming for some weeks the location shots for the English film *Richard III*. They came back as they promised during their quick visit to determine the location in the middle of August. They were ready to take advantage of the scenery, and above all, the weather –the sky!– of our country, which allows them to work continuously without suffering the inconveniences of their harsh weather. There is a nearly impassable barrier surrounding these two great artists and their "crew". On their quick visit to Madrid, they were able –not to remain incognito although they tried– to remain isolated from fans, curious people and journalists. Some journalists chatted with them –we were amongst the lucky ones– and some photographer took a picture of them. Warning: Although the couple is "inseparable", only the husband "works" on the film. (Cinema's mixed table, 1954)

Some images leaked from the shooting are reproduced in this chapter. All of them are by Norman Hargood, responsible for the Still Photography.

Olivier with Tony Bushell (above and below) and Pamela Davis [Continuity]

Sir Laurence Olivier in Spain

SIR LAURENCE'S DIARY

Finally, thanks to Olivier's concise diary, we know first-hand about the planning of the film:

On 2nd and 3rd September, Olivier visited El Campillo to take some shots (apparently, Vivien had planned to visit Barcelona on 3rd September but she remained in Paris). On 4th September, after lunch with Luis Roberts, he visited Aranjuez. On 5th September, he completed the location plotting. On 6th September, he worked on the script. That same day, Roger Furse –the Production Designer– arrived in Madrid. On 7th September, Olivier visited the location and wrote down the name of Sevilla Film Studios; Dr Torroba (the physician who extracted the arrow) and Francisco Prósper (the Set Designer) worked in this studio. There was a clear connexion, then, between *Richard III* and the studio, even though they only filmed on location.

The following is a time-line derived from the diary:

Frame of *Richard III*

- 8th September: more crew members arrive: Alex (Korda?), Cecil Tennant (Olivier's agent), and Carmen Dillon (the artistic director)
- 11th September: Vivien arrives in Madrid,
- 12th September (Sunday): shooting begins with the scenes "shadow", "Lords ride" and "Stanley note."
- 13th September: "Stanley's camp" is shot.
- 14th September: "Bosworth" is filmed,
- 15th and 16th September: several scenes from "Henry's camp" are shot.
- 17th September: Olivier writes "The Arrow" enclosed in brackets, which suggests that the arrow scene was filmed together with King Richard reciting "Our ancient word of courage, fair Saint George" (in his diary, though, he only writes the words "Word o Steam"). If this is the day he was injured, he does not mention it, and the shooting of additional scenes continues trouble-free in the following days.
- 20th September: shooting resumes.
- 21st September: Norfolk's scene on the bridge is completed.
- 18th, 20th and 21st September: an extra note ("dele") probably indicates that some scenes were cut.
- 22nd September, scenes at Richard's camp and "Catesby & Rat" are filmed.
- 23rd September: more scenes in the camp are shot, together with Stanley's scenes and the first-night shooting.
- 24th September; Olivier writes "'Montage' Army"; probably the first day of work with the Spanish extras/soldiers.
- 25th September: they shoot scenes of Richard with the ghosts,
- 27th September: some battle scenes are mentioned ("Battle's Split Seven").
- 28th September: Richard's visions are filmed, and some shots from the crane are taken.
- 29th September, more battle scenes
- 30th September, scenes of Richard's right flank.

- 1st October: the charge is filmed.
- 2nd October: close shots of the horse's mêlée.
- 4th October, the impressive scene of the crown kicking is shot, along with horses from the crane and Richard reciting "Come, bustle; bustle; caparison my horse."

Tuesday, 5th October 1954, the last day of shooting, finds the diary full of notes. There was a retake, and Olivier drew a cross (probably the one from the Valley of Fallen, mentioned above). They also shot another scene titled "Honi Soit" (a sentence not from *Richard III* but from *The Merry Wives of Windsor*[14]), in addition to the scene of the crown on the bush and others. Finally, they ended filming at 11 pm.

---

[14] "Honi soit qui mal y pense".

Olivier and crew in the tower where they will film the battle scenes

On 6th October in the afternoon, Olivier departed from Barajas and he mysteriously wrote in his diary the word "Othello" next to Luis Roberts' name. Did they possibly discuss a future film about *Othello*?

What Olivier indeed would try to put together two years later was a filmed version of *Macbeth* with Vivien Leigh, after their successful season at the 1955 Stratford Festival. There is a script with Olivier's notes for future shooting, and in the summer of 1958 he searched for locations in Scotland; this time he wanted to make a 'realistic' version. But the retirement of Filippo Del Giudice (the producer of

Henry V and *Hamlet*) to Italy left Olivier without funding, and none of the studios dared to risk money (Korda had died in 1956). Thus, the project, unfortunately for any cinema and theatre lovers, was aborted.

COMPARATIVE

A frame of *Richard III* and a photograph taken by the author in 2012. The cross of the Valley of the Fallen can be seen at the top left of the images

A frame of *Richard III* and a photograph of the same mountain range

A frame of *Richard III* and a photograph of a similar rock formation near Galapagar

THE FILM IN THE SPANISH CINEMAS

Richard III premiered in the Lope de Vega cinema in Madrid, amongst other places, on 30th December 1957 and in the Tívoli cinema in Barcelona on 27th January 1958. In the Primer Plano magazine review, the shooting in Spain was briefly mentioned but this fact was never used to promote the film.

A rare Spanish poster where the battle scene is shown

5. DALÍ'S PORTRAIT[15]

In April 1955, Alexander Korda, *Richard III*'s producer, commissioned Salvador Dalí –who already had an international recognition as a painter– to paint Laurence Olivier's portrait for publicity purposes.

Laurence Olivier and Salvador Dalí chat before one of their sessions

The portrait was painted during several sessions at the Claridge Hotel in London. For one of these sessions, the press had free access, so photographs of Dalí and Olivier together memorialize the

---

[15] Although the portrait was painted in London, the author includes the chapter due to its Costa Brava connection.

event. Always an eccentric character, Dalí did not disappoint during their last session: Once he finished his work, Dalí unrolled a sheet of paper, made two little dots on it, and walked away.

Dalí completed the portrait in his studio in Port Lligat (Girona). When the portrait was about to be shipped to London, Barcelona Airport Customs detained the painting and it was declared a national work of art. By the time the painting arrived at Korda's London Films, it was too late to use it for promotion, the sole purpose for its commission.

About the later whereabouts of the portrait, there exist two totally opposed versions.

According to the first version –appearing in Tarquin Olivier's biography and in Olivier's official biography by Terry Coleman– Olivier kept the portrait. Tarquin talks about Dalí's portrait of Richard III hanging on the wall behind Olivier, in his Brighton house (bought in the early 60s). And Coleman says:

> He had sold the portrait of him as Richard III by Salvador Dalí [to pay his children's school fees]. It had been done rapidly, in a few sittings at Claridge's in 1955, after his great success in the film [and was given to Olivier by Alex Korda]. It shows him both in full face and in profile and is a sensational portrait, not at all subtle, but after that of him as a young Romeo it was his favourite. He had kept it illuminated on the walls of his dining room at Brighton and had always been peculiarly possessive of it. He had earlier not even replied to the Dalí Museum's request for information about it and, in response to an American authority on the painter, had got his secretary to reply merely that he had been much excited to sit for Dalí, who was a genius. What more, he asked, could be said? But early in 1989 the painting was sold at Sotheby's for L396,000. It went to the Dalí Museum in Barcelona [sic] (Coleman, 2005).

The second version, which appeared in Peter Moore's obituary from El País newspaper, reads:

> Korda sent his right-hand man, Peter Moore, to meet Dalí to negotiate the fee for the painting. Captain Moore kept the oil painting "Portrait of Laurence Olivier in the role of Richard III" until 2000 when the Dalí Foundation bought it for half a million dollars. Nowadays it can be seen at the Dalí Museum in Figueres (El País, 2005).

Today, the painting is, indeed, a property of the Dalí Museum in Figueres, but it is not on permanent display as it travels to different exhibitions.

The official Salvador Dalí site lists its provenance as Sir Alexander Korda, London / Sir Laurence Olivier, London / The Lefevre Gallery, London / Peter Moore, Cadaqués / Auctioned at Sotheby's, London December 7th, 1999.

6. CHRISTMAS IN ANDALUSIA

After the shooting of *Richard III*, the Oliviers –who usually spent their holidays in Italy– started to consider Spain a holiday destination as well.

But they only visited it once more. During the 1956 Christmas season, Olivier was exhausted after shooting *The Prince and the Showgirl* (1957) with Marilyn Monroe, and was also suffering a gout attack. Thus, he followed his friends' recommendation –Dr Seidmann and his wife, Ginette Spanier– and flew with Vivien from London to Gibraltar on 22nd December 1956. From there they travelled to Torremolinos, where they stayed at the now closed Playa Hotel until 15th January 1957.

The Oliviers pictured in the Playa Hotel

Map of the zone with the towns mentioned encircled in red

In his memoirs, Olivier confessed that he and Vivien were embarrassingly quarrelsome most of the time and that the poor Seidmanns had a miserable holiday. In a postcard to Tarquin, he related that he had swum three times in the 'diamond cold' water, despite his gout and some stomach problems.

This visit of the couple was better documented by the Spanish press. At the beginning of January, the Oliviers gave a brief interview to some journalists from Madrid. That day, local journalists from Sur newspaper (thanks to Mr. Marquez –the Torremolinos superintendent– and the son of the hotel owners) also had access to the "stars". The interview appeared in triplicate at Diario Sur, Sábado Gráfico and Primer Plano magazines.

VIVIEN LEIGH Y LAURENCE OLIVIER, EN TORREMOLINOS.—La pareja cinematográfica más famosa de Europa se ha trasladado a Torremolinos para descansar unos días. Constaba en su programa sendos viajes a Sevilla y a Granada, después de un breve reposo en la Costa del Sol. Vivien y su marido han hecho unas declaraciones especiales para nuestros lectores, que publicamos en el interior de este número.—Fotos Serrano.

Cover of *Sábado Gráfico*

ABC newspaper also provided briefs about two of their trips: to Seville (09/01/1957) and Cádiz (10/01/1957). The different interviews disclose what other places in Andalucía they visited: Córdoba, Ronda, Granada, Marbella, Mijas, Estepona, Gibraltar, Benalmádena, Churriana, Fuengirola, and Málaga (in Málaga they had lunch at Gibralfaro hostelry). They also made time for more flamenco, this time at the small and popular palace of the flamenco dancer Lola Medina in Torremolinos, where they could enjoy a private session from Antonio, the famous dancer.

The interview, mostly in French –Vivien Leigh spoke French fluently– and in English, was conducted with the help of José María Pérez Casero, a businessman from Málaga who acted as a translator. The couple was interviewed separately and Leigh, as usual, was shown in a better light than her husband by the Spanish press. No scoop or remarkable comment came from the couple, but it is curious to read that they saw *Marcelino Pan y Vino*[16] (1955) three times (and without speaking Spanish, of course).

Here are both interviews from Diario Sur.

Interview with Vivien Leigh [Sur - 08/01/1957]

We arrived in a big DKW car at the Playa Hotel. We were interested and curious, and finally we were able to speak with Sir Laurence Olivier and Vivien Leigh. As ladies come first, today's article is dedicated to kind Vivien, to whom we could speak from time to time in French, as she speaks very good French.

The *Gone with the Wind* star has a wonderful personality. She is the same woman we see on the screen. Beautiful, with shining green eyes and a slight figure, modestly and elegantly dressed in a grey dress and a suede coat.

We want to know why they came to Malaga.

---

[16] *Miracle of Marcelino*, an internationally successful Spanish film (religion themed).

- Some friends who live in Marbella spoke to us about Malaga. And we are delighted to be here. We have visited a lot of towns: Ronda, Mijas, Marbella, and Estepona. We have reached Gibraltar, Benalmádena, and I've been very impressed with all of them due to their originality and contrast.

Vivien Leigh, daughter of military officers, was born in Bombay[17] [sic], and she has a long and successful career, but we want to know what her favourite films are.

- *Gone with the Wind* and *A Streetcar Named Desire*. By the way, they have told me that, in Spain, my films are shown with a lot of cuts.

- It's true –we answer her.

And we don't know anything else to say. We know they are cut. But we ignore the reason. Maybe it's because their excess of dialogue, of action, or acting or whatever. Or maybe it's because they are too long, like *The Wind*[18].

She speaks French very fast, and it's difficult for us to understand her. More slowly, we ask her.

And she agrees. We learn that she had performed *A Streetcar Named Desire* previously on stage, and this is the reason she is especially fond of this film.

- What role would you like to perform? Maybe Jeanne d'Arc?

- No. I like them all to be different. Many actresses have portrayed Jeanne d'Arc. I would like to do something new.

We suggest our saint from Avila, Saint Teresa, the walker and founder nun, who had such a big personality. She seems interested as it is her husband, Sir Laurence Olivier, who tries to catch the few things we can say in French about the saint.

- What kind of life do you have when you are not working?

---

[17] Vivien Leigh was born in Darjeeling (India).
[18] Censorship in Spanish cinema was due to moral or political subjects believed to be "dangerous" by the Franco's regime. The journalist was obviously avoiding the real reasons.

- A very quiet life. I like to rest. Home, sweet home. And I like to travel and discover beautiful towns like the Andalucía ones.

Their life here is indeed very relaxed. They rest until midday at their room, which has a wonderful terrace facing the sea, warmed all day by the sun. In the afternoons, they go on a trip with the French producer and his wife Mrs. Seidmann, or they play cards and go to sleep early at night. At midnight, they are in bed. Simple life. And no special food. They eat what the hotel offers them; there is no vegetarian nonsense.

By the way, we know that the actor and his wife were at Lola Medina's house. There they met Antonio, the famous flamenco dancer, and they saw him dancing in a very private show. It was so private that we didn't even get a picture for the press. (...)

- Are you thinking of giving up acting due to your home duties?

- Not at all. Home hasn't taken away a molecule of my enthusiasm for art.

- Who is the best director you've ever had?

She looks at Sir Laurence. They look each other, and they smile.

- My husband.

She is right. And Sir Laurence will never find a better actress than her to direct.

We want to know who have been her best partners at theatre or cinema, but she avoids answering because she says it is a very personal question.

The conversation acquires a general-interest tone. We want to know her opinion about Spain, about the Spanish people. The one she had in mind before visiting us.

And she makes it clear that she hadn't any prejudice. Her impression of Spain and the Spanish people is very good.

We talk about the world situation. We are living in dangerous times where anyone can blow the fuse that will explode the terrible powder keg that is our world right now.

- Are you afraid of the world news?

- Of course. Nobody can be happy with the current world situation.

And then we move into a more complicated conversation. Vivien says, more or less, that the artists owe allegiance only to their art. And that their opinions, about vital problems for humanity, are so private that they can't be expressed in public. And nothing else is said: her art is above everything else.

Interview with Laurence Olivier [Sur - 09/01/1957]

When we travelled to talk with them, they were waiting in the garden of the Playa Hotel for two journalists from Madrid who were coming to take pictures and to interview them. Luckily, we were assisted –we want to note our thanks– by the Torremolinos superintendent and Quique Bolín. After waiting a few minutes, the two stars came down together with their friend, the doctor and cinema producer Mr Seidmann. In the beginning, we had the impression that we would only meet the star of *Rebecca*, and not kind Vivien. Sir Laurence, who has been knighted recently by Her Gracious Majesty, is a man of concentrated expression. He is quite sparing with words, quite frugal with gestures. We had to win him over from the beginning, so we had to use old tricks; in this case, they weren't tricks but reality.

- Sir –we told him through our friend Pérez Casero–, it would be unthinkable that the present genius of the cinema and theatre would escape from the Malaga journalists without saying a word.

Then he smiled slightly, he shook our hand and invited us to sit down. He would give us an interview of five minutes. Only five minutes.

The good thing is that we were the only ones to interview him. And while we were chatting, more than twenty people surrounded us. From a window on the first floor, a French woman was filming the interview with her home movie camera. That was the reason Sir Laurence was hiding his face, so "madam's" film probably didn't completely capture the face of the star of the Shakespearian trilogy in cinema and theatre.

- Sir, what were you looking for in our city?

- I came looking for sun, peace and tranquillity.

We have evidence that he has found them all. Despite some early grey days, the rest of the time has seen lovely sunny days and, for this reason, he has abandoned the stick he needed to walk with. The British blood of Sir Laurence has already received the beneficial influence of the Andalusia sun.

- Are you working on something; do you have new projects?

- Nothing. I'm resting right now, and I'm not working at all.

For this reason, he is staying at Malaga; and our land and the weather are praised, frugally, by the famous actor and director. Like his wife, he is keen on all the towns they have visited in this province. And they have had a great time because they have friends all along the Costa del Sol and Torremolinos, so the rest has been combined with friendship.

Being European we ask him a decisive question,

- Which cinema do you consider superior, the European or the American one?

But the actor doesn't want to get into complications or to extend the interview and he says:

- It's very difficult to answer this question.

(...)

- Which do you prefer: directing or acting?

- In cinema, I prefer directing. And in the theatre, I prefer acting. (This opinion is shared by most of the actors. The warmth from the public's approbation is preferable to the monotonous repetition of the scenes at a movie set, in front of a director).

- Who do you like to direct best: men or women?

- I don't have any preferences. Depends on the person, I must say, on the art or the flexibility of this person.

- And in all your extensive life as a director, who is the best actor or actress you have ever directed?

Now the "gentleman", the *Sir*, appears. He considers it wouldn't be diplomatic to answer that. He says it wouldn't be kind for some people and that he prefers to remain silent. And he does it. Another question is the future of the cinema and the theatre, threatened by that mighty adversary who lives in every house, the television. The cinema has defended itself with the colour, the relief, the cinemascope. It doesn't want to die.

Sir Laurence agrees with us. He doesn't have arguments to answer the question, but he sees this mighty enemy as a big danger.

We move on; Spanish cinema.

- I've seen a Spanish movie: *Marcelino Pan y Vino*.

- We have seen it three times –says Vivien.

- And I quite enjoyed it –continues Sir Laurence–. I think that Spanish cinema, judging by this movie, has lots of possibilities.

Time is running out. The sun is setting behind the Mijas mountain range. We look at our watch, and we see his polite gesture. We finish the interview.

- What hobbies do you have when you are not working on cinema or theatre?

- I enjoy gardening.

And the last question. This one is from Smerdou, who has been at the interview with us and who knows a lot about cinema.

- Is the film *The Sleeping Prince*[19] already finished?

Smerdou expected another answer, but the actor answers as concisely and calmly as he did the other questions:

- It's totally finished. Only some music arrangements remain to be done.

If the readers don't understand Guillermito's question, they should know that this modern genius of the cinema has recently done a film with the genius of American cinema architecture, Marilyn Monroe.

The talk ends in the usual way. We say goodbye, and we thank him for his kindness:

- We think you are an excellent actor, director and person.

He smiles, and Vivien too. Vivien's smile lights up the scene.

---

[19] Later known as *The Prince and the Showgirl*.

The Oliviers and the Seidmanns visiting Málaga

They ended their vacation by flying from Málaga ("trouble over seat at airport" wrote Olivier in his diary) to Madrid. They stayed at the Ritz Hotel, visited the Prado Museum, and bought art objects. Again, they gave a few minutes to the press. Their interview was summarized in the following points and published in the Portuguese magazine Plateia:

- We prefer theatre to cinema. But films have given us more fame and money.
- Torremolinos is full of air, sea, pines and tranquillity.
- Only the soundtrack is left to complete the production of *The Sleeping Prince*, a film that has caused Sir Laurence – according to himself– a lot of headaches and problems.
- Hollywood doesn't entice us and we think the movie industry in the film capital of the world is in trouble. The main causes are an alarming lack of good plots and the quality of the European cinema, which gets better and better. Not to mention television.

- We like paintings and music. We like to visit good museums and to attend important concerts by the great geniuses.
- We hate publicity, and we prefer to avoid journalists... at least most of the time.

The Oliviers check the newspapers during their brief stay in Madrid

During this quick visit to Madrid, in January 1957, Olivier probably gave an interview to TVE (the Spanish National Television), the only existing TV channel in those days. The only evidence we have of it is a comment from the late journalist Tico Medina:

> While he was waiting for the British Ambassador's Rolls Royce, at the door of the Paseo de la Habana studios in Madrid after the interview, Laurence Olivier told us —strongly shaking our hands with amazement: "Congratulations, congratulations... I congratulate you because it's a miracle; you are making television in a shoe box." (Medina, 1996)

These would be the last vacation the Oliviers took together. In 1957, their marriage, intermittently in crisis, fell apart.

7. OTHERS VISITS TO SPAIN

The very first visit of Sir Laurence Olivier to Spain, even though it is briefly documented, occurred in February 1948. After finishing his *Hamlet,* Olivier, together with Vivien Leigh and a part of the Old Vic Theatre Company, set out on a long voyage from England to Australia and New Zealand. There, they performed three plays from their repertoire over several months. According to a brief note published in Primer Plano magazine on 29th February 1948, the company's ship had a stop or a layover at the Canary Islands: "The Spanish readers from the Canary Islands have been lucky to see him".

On September 1958, Olivier travelled with his brother Dickie and his sister-in-law Hester to the Costa Brava, probably to S'Agaró –a luxurious residential area that became internationally famous in the 50s. His brother was terminally ill with leukaemia, so Olivier intended to spend some holiday days with him and his wife, but he had to return to England unexpectedly: Vivien Leigh was experiencing a new crisis brought on by her bipolar disorder.

Laurence Olivier and Vivien Leigh were divorced in 1960. In 1964 Olivier, with his new wife, the actress Joan Plowright, and their children Richard and Tamsin –Julie Kate would be born later on– travelled to the Balearic Islands. It was a place they would visit on several occasions.

At the end of September 1964, Olivier was spotted by El Mundo Deportivo newspaper –back then it wasn't only a sports newspaper– at the Majorcan beach of Formentor. The family stayed at the exclusive Formentor Hotel, and enjoyed swimming in the Mediterranean Sea. The actor even dared to practice water-skiing. They also witnessed the filming of the Spanish film *Playa de Formentor* (Formentor's Beach) starring Margit Kocsis, a Hungarian-Dutch painter and actress. El Mundo Deportivo didn't get photos of

Olivier, but the script girl did; she photographed him in "green trunks".

On 20th September, the Sunday Mirror published a small article about his Majorcan holidays together with some new, and unusual, photographs of Olivier playing with his children on the beach.

Front page of Sunday Mirror

Formentor Beach (above) and the entrance of the exclusive Formentor Hotel (below) in 2012

In 1965 (and maybe as early as 1964) the Oliviers visited Ibiza, staying at the small town of Santa Eulària des Riu. According to the Daily Mail, Olivier's visit to Ibiza secured Ibiza's reputation as the most fashionable place in Europe. It so happened that the only telephone in Santa Eulària was in Sandy's Bar (managed by a British man), so dozens of celebrities visited this bar: Olivier, Errol Flynn, Denholm Elliot, Leslie Philips, Terry Thomas, Nigel Davenport, Diana Rigg, John Mills, Terence Stamp or Freddy Mercury.

In August 1968, the Olivier family spent four weeks of vacation in Spain but precisely where remains unknown.

After several illnesses –amongst them prostate cancer in 1968– Olivier was thinking about retiring, and he spent a long stay in Santa Eulària, from August to October 1970.

In 1971, despite being ill again, Olivier made a two-day trip –this time for professional reasons– to the Costa Brava. He was there from 13th to 15th April to film a few scenes for the film *Nicholas and Alexandra* by Peter Shaffer as the secretary to the Tsar at La Gavina Hotel in S'Agaró.

Frame of *Nicholas and Alexandra*

The Spanish press mentioned his visit only after the actor had returned to England.

During the mid-70s, Olivier did an unaccredited visit to Barcelona, together with the film director John Schlesinger and John Gielgud. The three of them went to a night club and got drunk. Olivier dropped his glass over Gielgud and Gielgud, totally intoxicated, stood up and in a 'bitchy' impersonation of Olivier, started to declaim "Out, damned spot! Out, I say!" from the Scottish play.[20]

There are, also, some accounts of Olivier and Plowright visiting the Spanish actress and director Núria Espert and her husband, the director Armando Moreno, at their holiday home in Alcossebre (Castelló). In 1986, Espert directed Joan Plowright and Glenda Jackson at *The House of Bernarda Alba* in London.

Olivier's last recorded visit to Spain took place during April-May 1988, one year prior to his death. Already very ill, he spent three weeks in a villa near Marbella with his wife Joan and a nurse. During his stay, on one occasion, they drove along the winding road to Ronda; it was the same road that he and Vivien Leigh had driven along thirty years before.

---

[20] John Schlesinger told this anecdote to the Spanish film critic Fausto Fernández.

8. ILLUSTRATIONS

Cover: © Norman Hargood // Back cover: Serrano/Salas

Chapter 1: Felix H. Man
London Films

Chapter 2: *Triunfo* (Basabe)

Chapter 3: *Primer Plano* (EFE)
La Actualidad Española (Leal)
Magazine La Vanguardia
Primer Plano (CIFRA)
Fotogramas (Salgado)

Chapter 4: Google Maps
Universitas Nebrissensis
Djaa. Solo cultura, Valencia y Benimàmet
London Films
© Norman Hargood (2)
Primer Plano (Martín)
Primer Plano (Saiz)
© Norman Hargood (3)
London Films & © Margarida Araya (3)
Primer Plano

Chapter 5: Pictorial Press
© Salvador Dalí, Fundació Gala-Salvador Dalí

Chapter 6: Serrano/Salas
Google Maps
Sábado Gráfico (Serrano)
Primer Plano (Salas)
Plateia

Chapter 7: Sunday Mirror (Tom Blau)
© Margarida Araya (2)
Horizon Pictures

9. BIBLIOGRAPHY

ABC. (1954). Laurence Olivier y Vivien Leigh, a Madrid. (13 Aug.).

———. (1954). Mesa revuelta del cinematógrafo. (6 Oct.).

———. (1955). ABC en Londres: La batalla de Bosworth en Torrelodones. (16 Dec.)

———. (1959). News. (12 Sep.).

———. (1970). News. (4 Sep.).

———. (1971). News. (17 Apr.).

ABC Sevilla. (1954). Visita a Madrid de sir Lawrence Olivier. (14 Aug.).

———. (1957). Lawrence Olivier y su esposa, Vivien Leigh, en Sevilla. (10 Jan.).

———. (1957). Laurence Olivier y Vivien Leigh, a Cádiz. (11 Jan.)

Andresco, V. (1954). Sir Laurence Olivier y Vivien Leigh hablan para Fotogramas. *Fotogramas*. (20 Aug.).

Armstrong, S. (2004) Why the stars love Ibiza. *Daily Mail*. (16 Aug.).

Bardavio, J. (2009). Joaquín Ruiz-Giménez Cortés, un reformista contra el sistema. *El Mundo*. (28 Aug.).

Barreira. (1954). Pareja estupenda: Vivien y Sir Lawrence. *Primer Plano*. (22 Aug.).

Blanco Cabrera, A.C. (2010). *Aquel Torremolinos (1950-1957)*. [online] [visited in 2011] Not available.

Caldito, A. (2013) *Francisco Prósper y los efectos*. [online] Historias cinematográficas. [visited in 2014] Available at http://historias-cinematograficas.blogspot.com/2013/02/francisco-prosper-y-los-efectos.html

Coleman, T. (2005). *Olivier*. London: Bloomsbury.

Conejo Alonso, A. (1957). Sir Lawrence Olivier y Vivien Leigh buscan en Málaga el sol, la paz y la tranquilidad. *Primer Plano*. (13 Jan.).

Cot, L. (1964). Un "astro" internacional curiosea en bañador el rodaje de la película 'Playa de Formentor'. *El Mundo Deportivo*. (2 Oct.).

Cottrell, J. (1975). *Olivier*. London: Prencite-Hall.

De las Muelas, J. (2012). Pedro Chicote. *Magazine La Vanguardia*. (22 July).

De Madrid al cine. (2003). Madrid: Centro Cultural de la Villa de Madrid.

Diez, J. (2013). *Monasterio del Escorial*. [online] djaa [visited in 2016] Available at http://www.jdiezarnal.com/monasteriodelescorial.html

Donald. (1954). Lawrence Olivier y Vivian Leigh, en Madrid. *ABC*. (14 Aug.).

El País. (2005). John Peter Moore ex secretario de Salvador Dalí. *El País* (29 Dec.).

Ibiza A-Z. (2007-2011). *Sandy's Bar*. [online] [visited in 2011] Not available.

Jiménez Aguirre, J.M. (1957). Vivien Leigh y Laurence Olivier hablan para Sábado Gráfico. *Sábado Gráfico*. (12 Jan.).

La Vanguardia Española. (1954). Sir Laurence Olivier, en nuestra ciudad. (13 Aug.).

———. (1964). Sir Lawrence Olivier y su esposa, en Mallorca. (20 Sep.).

———. (1970). Sir Laurence descansa en Ibiza. (27 Aug.).

———. (1971). Lawrence Olivier ha filmado escenas de un filme en la Costa Brava. (16 Apr.).

Lozano, J.M. (1954). Scarlatta O'Hara y Hamlet, en Madrid. *La actualidad española*.

Marsillach, A. (1963). Vivien Leigh. Durante veinte años señora de Olivier. *Triunfo*. (12 Jan.).

Medina, T. (1996). *ABC*. (10 Nov.).

Morales, S. (1954). Vivien Leigh, por bulerías. El flechazo de Lawrence Olivier. *Primer Plano*, (9 Sep.).

Olivier, L. (1954) Diary. The British Library.

———. (1986). *On acting*. London: Sceptre.

Olivier, T. (1992). *My father Laurence Olivier*. London: Headline.

Pérez Lozano, J.M. (1954). Scarlatta O'Hara y Hamlet, en Madrid. *La actualidad española*. (19 Aug.).

Pita, E. (2007). El amigo español de Orson Welles y Ava Garder. *El Mundo*. (28 Jan.).

Primer Plano. (1948). Antes de pasar por España. (29 Feb.).

———. (1954) Sir Lawrence, brindis y ¡olé! (12 Sep.).

———. (1955). News.

Rueda, V. (1954). Lawrence Olivier y Vivien Leigh en Madrid. Vacaciones en busca de exteriores. *Primer Plano*. (22 Aug.).

Salvador Dalí (2014). *Richard the Third*. [online] Can Antaviana, S.L. [visited in 2016] Available at http://www.salvador-dali.org/cataleg_raonat/fitxa_obra.php?text=olivier&obra=712&lang=en

Serrano, A. (1957). O Casal Vivien Leigh Lawrence Olivier passa umas curtas férias em Espanha. *Plateia*. (1 March).

Sunday Mirror. (1964). Olivier and his family. (20 Sep.).

Tocildo, A. (1954). *Triunfo*. (23 June).

Trevor Bale, P. (n.d.). Richard III Society, American Branch.

Universitas Nebrissensis (2016). *La universidad*. [online] Universidad Nebrija. [visited in 2016] Available at http://www.nebrija.com/la_universidad/visita-virtual/galeria-instalaciones.php

Vickers, H. (1990) *Vivien Leigh*. London: Pan Books.

Yareham, R. (n.d.). *Silver Screen Spain*. [online] [visited in 2011] Not available.

Z. (1957). Para Vivien Leigh sus dos mejores películas han sido "Lo que el viento se llevó" y "Un tranvía llamado Deseo". *Sur*. (8 Jan.).

———. (1957). Sir Lawrence Olivier ha venido buscando a Málaga, el sol, la paz y la tranquilidad. *Sur*. (9 Jan.).

10. ABOUT THE AUTHOR

Margarida Araya (Barcelona, 1973) has a Bachelor Degree in Translation and Interpreting and a Master's in Theatrical Studies. Amongst her published works are *Timothy Dalton: A Complete Guide to his Film, Television, Stage and Voice Work* and the translation of the play *Frost/Nixon* by Peter Morgan. Margarida is an anglophile, a theatre-goer and a film buff, three passions that have led to her admiration for Laurence Olivier's persona and career. She is the administrator of the "Sir Laurence Olivier (fan page)" facebook page and twitter account and the webmistress of the Sir Laurence Olivier Stage Work site dedicated to Olivier's theatre career.

Printed in Poland
by Amazon Fulfillment
Poland Sp. z o.o., Wrocław